Something Spicy

Something

Illustrated by
MATTHEW WAWIÓRKA

Designed by
LYNETTE CORTEZ

Produced by
MILLER AND O'SHEA, INC.

SPICY

TEXT *and* RECIPES
by FRANCES TOWNER GIEDT

SIMON & SCHUSTER
New York London Toronto Sydney Tokyo Singapore

Simon & Schuster

Rockefeller Center

1230 Avenue of the Americas

New York, NY 10020

DESIGNED BY LYNETTE CORTEZ

Manufactured in the United States of America

1 3 5 7 9 10 8 6 4 2

ISBN: 978-1-4767-4562-6

To David,

my husband and best friend,

for adding spice to my life.

Contents

SPICY FROM THE STOVE-TOP

Introduction

JUST ENOUGH SPICE *for* EVERY CRAVING

Do you have the urge for a spicy snack? A craving for something with just a smidgeon of heat?

Do you prefer food that delivers a tantalizing carnival of zingy flavors? Or are you ready for a four-alarm fire in your mouth?

I have always loved spicy food. Growing up, I was the one reaching for the pepper shaker, sprinkling more chili 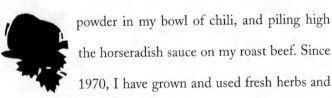 powder in my bowl of chili, and piling high the horseradish sauce on my roast beef. Since 1970, I have grown and used fresh herbs and chiles in my cooking. My spice collection, once housed in the basic 12-bottle spice rack, now fills an entire kitchen cabinet with exotic spices and spice blends lovingly collected from all over the world.

There's been a recent explosion of interest in spicy food. A stroll down the aisle of supermarkets across the country confirms this. At the same time, we are also aware that our food should be and can be more healthful.

Something Spicy is sure to offer something for everyone, then. Making use of a wide range of fresh, flavorful ingredients, here are recipes for zesty, mouth-watering snacks to munch in the morning, to  nibble in the mid-afternoon or to tease the appetite with cocktails before dinner -- a variety of snacks from mild to scorching, something for every mood. No matter what your preference is, you'll enjoy snacking your way through the sultry cuisines of the world -- Southwest, Cajun, Szechuan, Mexican, South American, Thai, Italian, and Middle Eastern.

Some of the recipes are so simple that they can be prepared in minutes. Others are substantial enough for a light meal. Several can be served sizzling from the barbecue, electric, or stove-top grill. And many are so lean and nutritious that you can indulge even while watching your diet. All are easy to prepare and fun to eat.

Many of the recipes get their fire from fresh chiles. If you're not used to cooking with fresh chiles, be careful. The same source of heat that inflames your mouth (an odorless substance called capsaicin that's concentrated in the veins and seeds of the chile) can do the same thing to your hands, eyes, and nose.  Always wear rubber gloves when working with fresh chiles and afterwards immediately wash your hands thoroughly with soap and water.

Not all of the dishes get their flavor kick from chiles. In several recipes, a more subtle spiciness comes from fresh ginger, mustard, or horseradish. Others use a combination of spices and herbs for their pungency. Just remember that everyone has a different level of tolerance for hot food -- what's meltdown for one is mild to another. But once you've braved the heat, you'll be back for more.

SETTING UP A SPICY PANTRY

A well equipped spice
pantry will ensure that your cooking
is never dull. Most of the staples for a spice
pantry can be found in larger supermarkets, ethnic stores,
and gourmet shops. You can also refer to the Source List
on page 96.

CHILES: You'll find several kinds of chiles, from mild
to scorching, used in this book. I keep dried habanero
chiles (the hottest chile in the world), dried New Mexican
red chiles (mild to medium-hot), dried hot pepper flakes
(medium-hot), and canned chipotles in adobo sauce (very
hot and smoky) on hand at all times.

Fresh chiles should be stored in the refrigerator, wrapped

in paper towels. Since their natural oils can irritate and burn the skin, be sure not to touch your face or eyes after handling fresh chiles. Always wash your hands after use. Keep these fresh chiles on hand: jalapeño (very hot), New Mexican green (medium to very hot), poblano (medium to hot), habanero, sometimes referred to as Scotch bonnet (extremely hot), and serrano (searing hot).

HERBS AND SPICES: Since dried herbs and spices lose their pungency quickly, write the date on the label when you open the jar and discard any unused portion after six months. You'll need cayenne pepper, a good-quality chili powder, a good-quality curry powder, ground cloves, ground cinnamon, ground cumin, ground nutmeg, mixed Italian herbs, dried oregano, and Szechuan peppercorns.

I have an extensive herb garden so fresh herbs are easily

available from spring through fall. To be ready for spicy cooking, you might want to grow basil, cilantro (fresh coriander), flat-leaf parsley, mint, oregano, and thyme in your own garden. During the winter months, you can buy fresh herbs at most large grocery stores. Year round, I buy fingers of fresh ginger.

SAUCES AND CONDIMENTS: Keep these on hand for spicy cooking: canned ripe olives, chunky-style peanut butter, Dijon mustard, jalapeño jelly, liquid hot pepper sauce, mango chutney, pimento-stuffed olives, soy sauce, sun-dried tomatoes, tahini, and wasabi powder.

BEANS AND OTHER LEGUMES: I store beans in glass jars with screw-on or clamp-on tops. You'll want on hand dried chick peas, dried red lentils, dried small red beans, and dried yellow split peas. Also stock canned black beans.

FLOUR AND GRAINS: Transfer grains and flour from their packaging to glass or plastic storage containers so you can dip in with a measuring cup or spoon. You'll be using all-purpose unbleached flour, instant polenta, quick-cooking couscous, quick-cooking oats, stone-ground cornmeal, and wheat germ.

NUTS AND SEEDS: The recipes call for a variety of nuts. Keep these on your shelf: almonds (whole blanched and sliced), pecan halves, pine nuts, pistachios (shelled and salted), walnut halves, coriander seeds, fennel seeds, pumpkin seeds, and sunflower seeds.

MISCELLANEOUS: Your spicy pantry should have at least one box, can, bottle, or package of dates, golden raisins, chicken stock, flaked unsweetened coconut, poppadums, semi-sweet chocolate chips, rice paper rounds, dried cherries or cranberries, and pure vanilla extract.

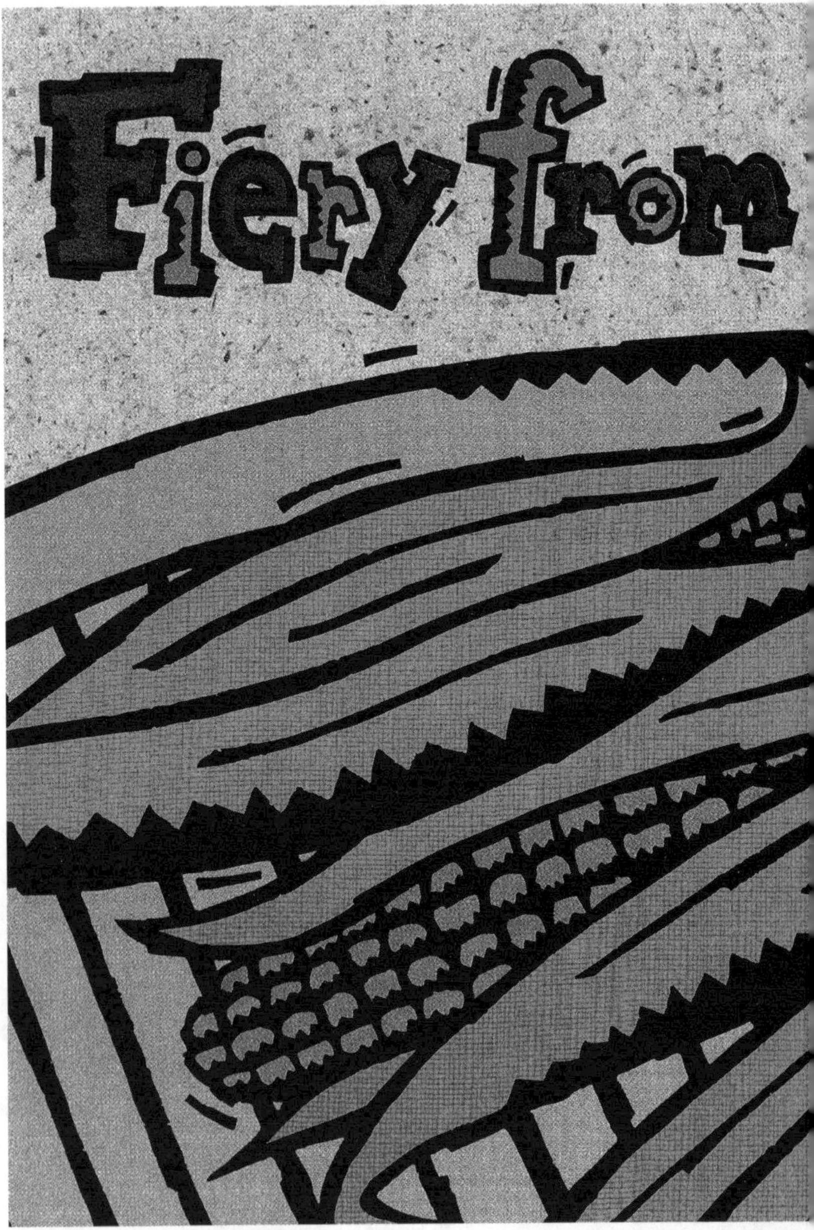
Fiery from

the Grill

BRUSCHETTA WITH CILANTRO PESTO

Makes 12 pieces
Time: 15 minutes

Grilling imparts a smoky flavor to thick slices of crusty Italian bread for this quick snack. The Cilantro Pesto adds a nice nip.

Cilantro Pesto
3 large garlic cloves, peeled and cut in half
3 tablespoons pine nuts
½ teaspoon salt
¼ cup grated Parmesan cheese
4 to 5 tablespoons olive oil
cup loosely packed fresh cilantro leaves

12 slices crusty Italian bread, sliced ½-inch thick
3 to 4 garlic cloves, cut in half
Olive oil for brushing

1. To prepare pesto, combine garlic, pine nuts, salt, and 1 tablespoon olive oil in the work bowl of a food processor or blender. Process until smooth. Add cilantro. Process for 15 seconds. Scrape down sides.

2. With motor running, slowly add remaining oil through feed tube. Process until smooth. Set aside. (Pesto will keep in the refrigerator for 2 days.)

3. For bruschetta, preheat a charcoal or gas grill. Over a medium-hot grill, toast bread slices until lightly browned on both sides, about 1 minute total. Rub a cut clove of garlic on one side of each slice, then brush with oil. Spread about 1 tablespoon pesto on each hot toast. Serve warm.

CHICKEN WINGS WITH CHIPOTLE PEANUT SAUCE

Makes about 30 pieces
Time: 60 minutes

Chipotle chiles, actually dried smoked jalapeños that are sold canned and packed in a spicy adobo sauce, a paste made up of ground chiles, herbs, and vinegar, add a fiery bite to this irresistible warm peanut dip. The chiles are available in the ethnic section of many supermarkets, specialty food shops, and by mail-order (see Sources, page 96). Canned green chiles could be substituted, but they'll provide a milder, different flavor.

2 pounds chicken wings, about 14 to 15 wings
Juice of 1 fresh orange
3 large garlic cloves, mashed
1 teaspoon liquid hot pepper sauce
1 teaspoon salt
1 teaspoon freshly ground pepper

Chipotle Peanut Sauce
4 large garlic cloves, minced
1 medium onion, finely chopped

1 tablespoon peanut oil
4 canned chipotle chiles in adobo, reserve adobo sauce
½ cup chunky-style peanut butter
½ cup chicken stock

1. Remove and discard wing tips. Split wings at the joint into 2 pieces. Place in a large glass, ceramic, or other non-aluminum shallow dish.

2. Combine orange juice, garlic, liquid hot pepper sauce, salt, and pepper. Pour over wings. Cover and refrigerate for at least 30 minutes, or up to 24 hours. Turn wings once or twice during marinating period.

3. Meanwhile, prepare the dipping sauce in a small metal saucepan that later can go directly on the grill. Mince garlic. Chop onion. Sauté garlic and onion in peanut oil over low heat until onion is soft but not browned, about 5 minutes.

4. In a food processor or blender, puree chipotles (reserve adobo sauce for later use), peanut butter, and stock. Add to onion mixture and cook, stirring, for 5 minutes until smooth and well blended. Stir in 1 tablespoon of reserved adobo sauce from the canned chipotles. Add more sauce to taste.

5. Remove wings from marinade. Set wings aside. Strain marinade into a small saucepan and cook over high heat until reduced by half.

6. Prepare a charcoal or gas grill. Brush wings with reduced marinade. Grill, 4 to 6 inches from heat source, turning several times, until wings are crispy and juices run clear, about 15 to 20 minutes. Keep sauce warm at the edge of the grill for dipping wings.

GRILLED POLENTA WITH HOT & WILD GUACAMOLE

Makes 8 pieces
Time: 35 minutes

Crisp on the outside, light and creamy inside, Italian polenta is transformed into a southwestern snack, first chili-seasoned, then grilled and topped with a spicy guacamole.

4 cups cold water
1 teaspoon salt
½ teaspoon chili powder
⅛ teaspoon cayenne pepper
1¼ cups uncooked instant polenta, or 1¼ cups
  stone-ground yellow cornmeal
3 tablespoons grated Parmesan cheese
1 tablespoon unsalted butter
Olive oil for brushing

Hot & Wild Guacamole
1 jalapeño chile, seeded and minced
1 garlic clove, minced

2 tablespoons minced onion (about ½ small onion)
1 tomatillo, husked and minced
2 tablespoons minced fresh cilantro
2 large ripe avocados
Juice of 1½ limes
¼ teaspoon liquid hot pepper sauce or to taste
Salt and freshly ground pepper to taste

1. In a saucepan, bring water to a boil. Stir in salt, chili powder, and cayenne pepper. Slowly add polenta. Stir in Parmesan
cheese and butter. Cook, stirring constantly, for 4 minutes.
2. Line a 9-inch square pan with plastic wrap. Spread hot
polenta mixture evenly in pan. Freeze for 15 minutes, or chill
in refrigerator for up to 24 hours.
3. Meanwhile, prepare guacamole. Mince and combine
jalapeño, garlic, onion, tomatillo, and cilantro. Peel and pit
the avocados; chop and mash them into a fine pulp. Add to
jalapeño mixture. Stir in lime juice and liquid hot pepper
sauce. Season with salt and pepper. Cover and chill until
ready to use.
4. Prepare grill or preheat broiler. Invert cooled polenta onto a
cutting board. Discard plastic wrap. Cut cooled polenta into 8
2¼-inch squares. Lightly brush each side with olive oil. Grill
or broil for about 5 minutes per side until lightly browned.
Serve topped with a generous dollop of guacamole.

JAMAICAN "JERKED" CORN ON THE COB

Makes 4 servings
Time: 50 minutes

The same aromatic seasoning that Jamaicans use on grilled meats and poultry shoots a peppery flavor kick into corn on the cob still warm from the field.

4 large ears fresh corn
1 Scotch bonnet or habanero chile, seeded and minced
1 large garlic clove, halved
2 tablespoons chopped fresh cilantro
½ tablespoon freshly ground pepper
1 teaspoon ground allspice
½ teaspoon salt
Juice of 1 lime
2 tablespoons unsalted butter

1. Prepare corn by pulling back husks without tearing to expose corn kernels. Remove all of the corn silk, brushing off any stubborn silks with your hand or a soft, dry vegetable brush. Replace husks over corn kernels. Soak in cold water for 20 to 30 minutes.

2. Meanwhile, start charcoal or gas grill. In the work bowl of a

food processor or blender, combine remaining ingredients and process to form a paste.

3. Remove corn from water. Pull back husks, blot dry with paper towels, and spread paste over corn kernels. Replace husks over corn kernels.

4. Grill, 4 to 6 inches from source of heat, turning frequently, for about 15 minutes. When done (corn kernels will give slightly under gentle pressure), remove husks. Serve hot.

PRAWNS WITH CHIMICHURRI SAUCE

Makes 4 servings
Time: 25 minutes

Use U-12 jumbo shrimp for this recipe, which are so nice and
large. You can also shake the Chimichurri Sauce, a spicy barbecue
sauce revered by Argentinean cowboys, over beef, chicken, pork,
or fish as it grills.

Chimichurri Sauce
1 cup coarsely chopped garlic, about 30 cloves
½ cup coarsely chopped fresh oregano
⅓ cup coarsely chopped fresh flat-leaf parsley
2 red serrano chiles, finely chopped
¼ cup sherry vinegar
1 cup olive oil

1 pound jumbo prawns
Grated zest of ½ lemon
Oil for brushing grill

1. Coarsely chop the garlic, oregano, and flat-leaf parsley.
Finely chop the serrano chiles. In a large bowl, whisk together
sauce ingredients. Peel and devein shrimp, leaving tails intact.
Add shrimp and lemon zest to sauce. Toss gently to coat each
shrimp. Marinate for 10 minutes.
2. Prepare charcoal or gas grill. Drain shrimp, reserving marinade. Place shrimp on a well-oiled grill, 4 to 6 inches from
source of heat. Cook, basting with reserved marinade, for
about 3 minutes per side, until shrimp are pink and opaque
throughout. Serve at once with sauce on the side.

Hot from

BABY POTATOES WITH FIERY HERBS

Makes about 3 dozen pieces
Time: 45 minutes

The humble potato becomes a scrumptious snack when roasted then tossed with garlic and pungent fresh herbs. Make lots -- they'll disappear quickly.

> 3 pounds very small white new potatoes (about
> 1 to 1½ inches in diameter), scrubbed
> 4 large garlic cloves, minced
> 4 fresh jalapeño chiles, minced
> ⅓ cup minced fresh cilantro
> ⅓ cup minced fresh oregano
> ⅓ cup olive oil
> ½ teaspoon coarse salt
> Freshly ground black pepper, to taste

1. Preheat oven to 375°. Prick potatoes with a fork and arrange in a large baking pan. Roast, uncovered, for 35 to 40 minutes, until potatoes are tender when pierced with a knife.
2. While potatoes are cooking, mince garlic, jalapeños, cilantro, and oregano.

3. Place roasted potatoes in a large bowl and while hot, toss with oil, salt, pepper, garlic, and jalapeños. Add cilantro and oregano and gently mix until evenly coated.

4. Arrange potatoes in a shallow serving bowl. Serve warm, speared with wooden cocktail sticks.

BACON WRAPPED DATES STUFFED WITH JALAPEÑO JACK CHEESE

Makes 24 pieces
Time: 45 minutes

Sweet dates, spicy melting cheese, and smoky bacon combine to make a quick, delicious snack.

6 ounces pepper Jack cheese, cut into 2 x ¼-inch pieces
24 large pitted dates
12 slices very thinly sliced lean bacon

1. Line a baking sheet with aluminum foil.
2. Slice the cheese. Stuff each date with a piece of cheese.
3. Cut bacon slices in half and wrap a slice around each stuffed date. Secure with a round wooden toothpick.
4. Place dates on the foil-lined baking sheet. Chill for at least 30 minutes.
5. Preheat oven to 400˚. Bake for 12 to 15 minutes, until bacon is crisp. Drain on paper towels. Serve warm.

BAKED CHIPS:

GARLIC HERB WONTON CHIPS

Makes about 90 chips
Time: 20 minutes

1 20-ounce package wonton skins
Water for spraying wonton skins
3 tablespoons grated Parmesan cheese
1½ teaspoons garlic powder
1 tablespoon mixed dried Italian herbs

1. Preheat oven to 375°.
2. Cut wonton skins in half diagonally and arrange in a single layer on an ungreased baking sheet. Using a sprayer or atomizer, mist wonton skins with water.
3. Combine remaining ingredients and sprinkle evenly over chips. Bake for 8 to 9 minutes, until lightly brown and crisp. (Chips will keep in an airtight container for up to 2 days.)

CUMIN PITA CHIPS

Makes 48 chips
Time: 25 minutes

6 tablespoons (¾ stick) unsalted butter
1 large garlic clove, minced
1 tablespoon ground cumin
3 6-inch pita breads
Coarse salt to taste

1. Preheat oven to 350°.
2. In a small saucepan, melt butter over low heat. Mince garlic and add to butter with cumin. Cook, stirring frequently, until garlic is soft but not browned, about 5 minutes.
3. Cut each pita bread into 8 wedges and separate each wedge into 2 triangles. Brush the butter lightly onto the rough side of each pita triangle.

4. Arrange triangles, buttered side up, on a large baking sheet. Sprinkle with salt. Bake for 12 to 15 minutes, until golden brown and crisp. (Chips will keep in an airtight container for up to 4 days.)

FENNEL PEPPER BAGEL CHIPS

Makes 96 chips
Time: 30 minutes

3 plain bagels
¼ cup (½ stick) unsalted butter
3 tablespoons fennel seeds or to taste
Freshly ground pepper to taste

1. Preheat oven to 325°. Melt butter in a small saucepan.
2. Cut each bagel in half vertically. Place each bagel half, cut side down, on a flat surface and cut each vertically into 8 slices.
3. Arrange bagel slices in a single layer on a large, ungreased baking sheet. Brush with butter. Sprinkle with fennel seeds and pepper. Bake for 20 minutes, until golden and crisp.
4. When cool enough to handle, break each bagel slice in half again. (Bagel chips will keep in an airtight container for up to 4 days.)

HEALTHY TORTILLA CHIPS (WITH SALSA)

Makes 96 chips
Time: 20 minutes

¼ teaspoon salt
1 teaspoon crushed dried oregano
½ teaspoon ground cumin
½ teaspoon cayenne pepper
12 6-inch fresh corn tortillas
Juice of 4 limes, strained

1. Preheat oven to 350°. In a small bowl, combine salt, oregano, cumin, and cayenne pepper. Set aside.

2. Cut each tortilla into 8 triangles. Pour strained lime juice in a sprayer or atomizer and mist tortilla triangles with juice. Sprinkle evenly with salt and herb mixture.

3. Bake for 10 to 12 minutes, until chips are crisp. Serve warm. (Store cooled chips in an airtight container for up to 1 day.)

SALSA

Makes about 3 cups
Time: 10 minutes

Salsa can be made out of most any fruit and many vegetables and combined with vinegar or citrus juice, chiles, onions, garlic, and cilantro or other pungent fresh herbs. The most familiar is this basic Southwestern tomato salsa.

3 large ripe tomatoes
2 fresh jalapeño chiles
1 small onion
1 large garlic clove
½ cup chopped cilantro
Juice of 2 limes
Salt and freshly ground pepper to taste

Dice tomatoes. Seed and mince jalapeños. Mince onion and garlic. Chop cilantro. Combine all ingredients. Cover and refrigerate until ready to use. (Will keep, refrigerated, for up to 2 days.)

BAKED QUESADILLA TRIANGLES WITH PINEAPPLE SALSA

Makes 6 servings
Time: 25 minutes

Goat cheese and fresh mint are a terrific combination in this quesadilla that oozes with luscious cheese and hot peppers. Serve it with a sweet-hot fruit salsa.

3 12-inch flour tortillas
1 cup shredded Jack cheese (about 4 ounces)
8 ounces fresh goat cheese, such as Montrachet, crumbled
½ cup coarsely chopped fresh mint
2 fresh jalapeño chiles, seeded and minced
3 scallions, white part and 1 inch green, minced

Pineapple Salsa
1 cup ripe, peeled, cored, and diced pineapple
1 fresh serrano chile, seeded and minced
3 scallions, white part and 1 inch green, minced
¼ cup minced red bell pepper (about ½ pepper)
Juice of 1 lime
2 tablespoons minced fresh mint

1. Preheat oven to 425°. Place a tortilla on a large baking sheet.
2. Shred Jack cheese. Combine with goat cheese. Spread half of the cheese mixture on the tortilla.
3. Chop mint. Seed and mince jalapeños. Mince scallions. Sprinkle cheese mixture with half of the mint, jalapeños, and scallions.
4. Place the second tortilla on top and spread with remaining cheese mixture. Top with remaining mint, jalapeño peppers, and scallions. Cover with the third tortilla. Loosely cover with foil.
5. Bake until heated through and cheese melts, 8 to 10 minutes.
6. While quesadilla bakes, prepare salsa. Peel, core, and dice pineapple. Seed and mince serrano chile. Mince scallions and red pepper. Combine with remaining salsa ingredients. Cut quesadilla into 6 wedges. Serve warm with salsa topping.

CAJUN CHEESE WAFERS

Makes about 24 wafers
Time: 45 minutes

These spicy cheese wafers are irresistible -- you can't eat just one. Keep a roll in your freezer ready to bake when friends stop by for a glass of wine or cocktails.

> 1 cup unbleached all-purpose flour
> ½ teaspoon salt
> ⅓ cup unsalted butter, softened
> 1 cup grated Parmesan cheese
> 1 large egg
> ½ cup finely chopped pecans
> Cayenne pepper

1. In a small bowl, combine flour and salt.
2. In a mixing bowl, beat together butter and Parmesan cheese. Add egg and beat until smooth. Gradually add flour mixture, mixing until well blended.
3. Divide dough in half and use your hands to shape each half into a smooth log about 1½ inches in diameter.
4. Finely chop pecans and place on a board or wax paper. Roll logs in pecans to coat sides evenly, pressing lightly to embed

nuts in dough. Wrap in wax paper or plastic wrap and freeze for 20 minutes.

5. Preheat oven to 375°. Slice dough into rounds about 1/4-inch thick. Place wafers 1 inch apart on ungreased baking sheets. Generously sprinkle tops with cayenne pepper. Bake for 10 to 12 minutes, until golden brown. Serve warm or at room temperature.

CHILE CHOCOLATE ALMOND COOKIES

Makes about 24 cookies
Time: 35 minutes

Chocolate and chiles?! The flavor combination found in Mexican mole is also delicious in a cookie.

1½ cups semisweet chocolate chips
¼ cup (½ stick) unsalted butter
¾ cup granulated sugar
1 large egg, slightly beaten
1½ teaspoons vanilla extract
¾ cup unbleached all-purpose flour
½ teaspoon salt
½ teaspoon ground cinnamon
¼ teaspoon baking powder
3 tablespoons crushed dried New Mexican red chiles
½ cup chopped almonds

1. Place 1 cup of the chocolate chips in a 1-quart, microwave-safe glass bowl. Microwave, uncovered, on medium (50 percent) power for 2 to 3 minutes, stirring after 2 minutes, until chocolate is smooth and melted. Be careful not to burn. (Or, melt in the top of a double boiler over simmering water.) Let cool.

2. Preheat oven to 350°. Lightly grease a cookie sheet.

3. In a large bowl, cream together butter and sugar. Slightly beat egg and add to butter mixture with vanilla extract. Stir in melted chocolate.

4. Combine flour, salt, cinnamon, and baking powder in a bowl. Gradually add to butter mixture, mixing well after each addition. Stir in chile pepper, almonds, and remaining ½ cup chocolate chips.

5. Drop batter in clumps of about 1 tablespoon each onto a lightly greased baking sheet, leaving about 2 inches between cookies. Bake for 8 to 10 minutes. Cool cookies on a wire rack.

CHILE, FETA CHEESE, AND WALNUT FILO BUNDLES

Makes about 60 pieces
Time: 45 minutes

These filo bundles, shaped like beggar's purses, bursting with cheese and hot chiles, are surprisingly easy to make.

> 1 New Mexican or Anaheim green chile, seeded and minced
> 2 scallions, white part and 1 inch green, minced
> ¼ cup chopped walnuts
> 1 large egg, lightly beaten
> 8 ounces feta cheese, at room temperature
> 1 teaspoon dried oregano, crushed
> ½ cup (1 stick) unsalted butter
> 1 pound filo pastry, 14 x 18 inches, thawed if frozen

1. Seed and mince chile. Mince scallions. Chop walnuts.
2. In a small bowl, lightly beat together egg and blend in cheese

until smooth. Stir in chiles, scallions, walnuts, and oregano.

3. Butter two large baking sheets.

4. Melt butter in small saucepan. Place 1 filo sheet on a smooth work surface (keep remaining filo covered with a slightly damp towel). Lightly brush filo sheet with butter. Cover with a second sheet of filo; lightly brush with butter. Top with a third sheet and again lightly brush with butter. Using a sharp knife, cut filo stack lengthwise into 4 strips, 3 ½ inches wide. Cut strips crosswise into 3½-inch squares.

5. Place 1 teaspoon cheese filling in the center of each square. Gather the edges together over the center, twisting them slightly to form a frill.

6. Transfer to prepared baking sheets, placing bundles 1 inch apart. Brush tops with melted butter. Repeat process using remaining filo sheets and cheese mixture.

7. Refrigerate for a least 1 hour before baking. (The bundles can be made up to a day ahead, covered with plastic wrap and refrigerated.)

8. When ready to bake, preheat oven to 350°. Bake bundles until golden brown and crisp, about 20 minutes. Cool 5 minutes before arranging on a serving platter.

FIERY PERSIAN SNACK MIX

Makes 4 cups
Time: 60 minutes

A colorful, highly seasoned mix of legumes for healthy munching.

> 1 cup dry chick peas
> 1 cup dry small red beans
> 1 cup dry red lentils
> 1 cup dry yellow split peas
> 9 tablespoons olive oil
> 2 teaspoons salt
> 1 teaspoon ground cumin
> 1½ teaspoons cayenne pepper
> ½ teaspoon garlic powder

1. Sort chick peas and beans for debris and rinse under cold running water. Place in a 3-quart saucepan. Cover with water and bring to a boil over high heat. Partially cover and cook until just barely tender, about 20 minutes. Drain and cool. Dry thoroughly on paper towels.

2. Meanwhile, sort and rinse lentils and split peas under cold running water. Place in a 2-quart saucepan. Cover with cold

water and bring to a boil over high heat. Partially cover and cook until just barely tender, about 5 minutes. Drain and cool. Dry thoroughly on paper towels.

3. Preheat oven to 375°. Combine oil and seasonings in the bottom of a large metal baking pan. Stir in legumes. Bake, stirring every 5 minutes, until legumes are crisp and chick peas are golden brown, 20 to 25 minutes. Serve warm, or store in an airtight container for up to 1 week.

GARLICKY ROASTED EGGPLANT WITH TOASTED PITA BREAD

Makes about 2 cups dip
Time: 60 minutes

This robust dip can also be spread on crusty peasant bread. The roasting smokes the eggplant, and tames and sweetens the garlic.

2 medium eggplants, about 1¼ pounds total
1 small, firm head of garlic, about 12 cloves
3 tablespoons olive oil
½ teaspoon salt
Freshly ground pepper
¾ cup soft breadcrumbs
Juice of 1½ lemons
3 tablespoons tahini

¼ teaspoon ground cumin
6 8-inch pita breads, cut into wedges and toasted
2 tablespoons chopped fresh parsley

1. Preheat oven to 350°. Place whole, unpeeled eggplants and garlic head on a large baking tray. Drizzle 1 tablespoon olive oil over garlic head. Roast until eggplants and garlic are soft to the touch, about 30 minutes. Remove from oven. While still hot, remove skin from eggplant and puree flesh in a food processor or blender.

2. Separate garlic head into individual cloves. Squeeze out the pulp and add to eggplant puree. Add remaining 2 tablespoons olive oil along with the rest of the ingredients, except pita bread and parsley. Process until smooth.

3. Transfer mixture to a serving bowl. Cover and chill for several hours or overnight. (Or, "quick chill" in the freezer for 30 minutes, stirring every 10 minutes.)

4. Meanwhile, to prepare toasted pita bread, cut each bread into 8 wedges. Preheat oven to 300°. Spread pita wedges in a single layer on a large baking sheet. Toast for 10 minutes. Turn over each wedge and continue to toast for another 5 to 10 minutes, until crisp.

5. When ready to serve, chop parsley and sprinkle over eggplant mixture. Serve with toasted pita wedges.

HOT NUTS:

LEMON-SPICED PISTACHIOS

Makes 2 cups
Time: 25 minutes

These nuts are addictive, but don't try to make them in larger batches since they need lots of room for toasting.

> 2 cups shelled, salted pistachios
> ½ cup granulated sugar
> Grated zest of 2 lemons
> 1 teaspoon ground nutmeg
> 1 teaspoon ground cinnamon
> Generous pinch of ground cloves

1. In a large, nonstick sauté pan over medium heat, toast pistachios, stirring frequently, until hot and golden, about 5 minutes.

2. Sprinkle pistachios with remaining ingredients. Continue to cook, stirring continuously until sugar melts and coats the nuts.

3. Spread mixture on a sheet of aluminum foil. When cool, break nuts apart. (The pistachios can be stored in an airtight container at room temperature for up to 1 week.)

MOROCCAN PECANS

Makes about 2 cups
Time: 25 minutes

Sweet and seductive. A nibble worthy of your best sherry or champagne.

>2 tablespoons unsalted butter
>3 tablespoons granulated sugar
>1½ teaspoons salt
>1½ teaspoons freshly ground pepper
>½ teaspoon ground cloves
>2 teaspoons ground cinnamon
>½ teaspoon ground cumin
>2 cups pecan halves

1. In a large, heavy-bottom skillet, melt butter over medium-low heat. Stir in remaining ingredients except pecans. Cook, stirring constantly, until sugar dissolves, about 3 minutes.
2. Add pecans and cook, stirring gently, until pecans are coated and crispy, about 5 minutes.

3. Remove from heat and spread pecans on aluminum foil. Cool. (The nuts can be stored in an airtight container for up to 2 weeks.)

SZECHUAN WALNUTS

Makes about 2 cups
Time: 45 minutes

Szechuan peppercorns, coriander seeds, and cayenne pepper provide a one-two punch of fiery flavor to these nuts. Szechuan peppercorns are available in Asian markets, specialty food stores, and some supermarkets. For mail-order, see Sources (page 96).

> 1 tablespoon Szechuan peppercorns
> 2 tablespoons coriander seeds
> ½ teaspoon cayenne pepper
> 1½ cups confectioners' sugar
> 2 tablespoons cornstarch
> ⅛ teaspoon salt
> Finely grated zest of 1 orange
> 2 eggs whites, slightly beaten
> Juice of ½ orange
> 2 cups walnut halves

1. Preheat oven to 250°. Heat a small, heavy-bottom skillet over high heat. Add peppercorns and coriander seeds. Toast

spices, stirring constantly, until aromatic, about 2 minutes.
Transfer spices to a spice mill, blender, or food processor.
Process for 30 seconds. Add cayenne pepper; set aside.

2. Sift together confectioners' sugar, cornstarch, and salt onto a
large sheet of parchment paper or waxed paper. Stir in orange
zest and spices.

3. In a medium bowl, lightly beat egg whites and add orange
juice. Add walnuts and stir to coat nuts thoroughly. Roll each
nut in sugar mixture.

4. Lay nuts (do not allow nuts to touch) on a nonstick baking
sheet and bake for 20 to 25 minutes until crispy and dry. Cool.
(Store in a covered container for up to 1 week.)

INDIAN SPREAD WITH POPPADUMS

Makes about 2 cups spread
Time: 25 minutes

Poppadums, partially cooked flat bread available in Indian markets and many supermarkets, make a flavorful base for this Indian curry-flavored, seven-layer spread. You'll need to make the yogurt cheese ahead of time because it takes several hours to drain.

> 1½ cups yogurt cheese (see box)
> 2 teaspoons curry powder
> ¼ teaspoon cayenne pepper
> 4 slices bacon, cooked crisp and crumbled
> ¼ cup mango chutney
> ⅓ cup chopped walnuts
> ⅓ cup chopped cilantro
> 3 tablespoons flaked unsweetened coconut
> ¼ cup golden raisins
> 15 poppadums

1. In a medium bowl, combine yogurt cheese, curry powder, and cayenne pepper. Spoon into a shallow serving dish and

smooth top with a spatula.

2. Cook bacon until crisp. Drain on paper towels and crumble.

3. Remove fruit from chutney sauce and chop into small pieces. Return fruit to sauce and spread over yogurt cheese mixture.

4. Chop walnuts and cilantro separately and reserve.

5. To make layers, top cheese mixture first with coconut, then walnuts, raisins, and bacon. Sprinkle evenly with cilantro. Set aside.

6. To prepare flat breads, place three poppadums at a time in a microwave in a single layer on sheets of paper towels. Cook on high for 30 seconds. Rearrange poppadums and continue to cook on high for another 30 seconds until they are evenly puffed and no dark patches remain.

7. Serve the poppadums with the spread.

YOGURT CHEESE
Makes about 1½ cups

For yogurt cheese, drain 3 cups plain low-fat or nonfat yogurt in a cheesecloth-lined sieve suspended over a deep bowl. Refrigerate for several hours or overnight to allow whey to drip out. When yogurt has thickened to the consistency of soft cream cheese, scrape yogurt away from the cheesecloth and transfer to a covered container. Refrigerate until ready to use, draining off any liquid that accumulates. Yogurt cheese can be kept in the refrigerator for up to 1 week.

LIME PEPPER COOKIE CRISPS

Makes about 3½ dozen cookies
Time: 45 minutes

These cookies are just right when your urge for something hot also cries out for something sweet.

> Grated zest of 4 limes
> 1 tablespoon lime juice
> 1 ¼ cups sugar
> ½ cup (1 stick) unsalted butter
> 2 large eggs
> 3 cups unbleached all-purpose flour
> 2 teaspoons baking powder
> ½ teaspoon salt
> ½ tablespoon cayenne pepper

1. Preheat oven to 375°.
2. Grate zest from limes. Squeeze lime juice.
3. In a food processor or blender, combine lime zest and sugar, processing until well combined, about 20 seconds. Measure out ½ cup and set aside.

4. In a large mixing bowl, cream together remaining ¾ cup lime sugar and butter until fluffy. Slightly beat eggs into butter mixture with lime juice.

5. In a separate bowl, combine flour, baking powder, salt, and cayenne pepper. Stir flour mixture into butter mixture just until combined.

6. Using your hands, roll dough into 1-inch balls. Place on ungreased baking sheet, leaving 2 inches between each ball. If dough is too soft to roll, chill a few minutes.

7. Using a fork to make a cross-hatch pattern, flatten the balls to a ¼-inch thickness. Bake for 7 to 12 minutes in preheated oven, until barely brown. Transfer to wire racks and generously sprinkle each cookie with reserved lime sugar. Cool and store in an airtight container.

RARE BEEF WITH ORANGE RELISH ON BAGUETTE

Makes 4 to 6 servings
Time: 30 minutes

This is the ultimate sub sandwich. You can use deli-purchased roast beef or cold beef from a leftover fillet of beef or sirloin tip roast.

1 large French baguette, about 1 pound
1 large bunch fresh arugula, washed and crisped
1¼ pounds sliced rare cooked fillet of beef
  or top sirloin

Orange Relish
3 large navel oranges
¼ cup minced red onion (about ½ onion)
2 tablespoons minced fresh mint
2 tablespoons minced fresh cilantro
¼ cup thinly sliced pimento-stuffed olives
2 garlic cloves, minced

¼ teaspoon hot red pepper flakes, or to taste
1 tablespoon olive oil
Juice of 1 fresh lime

1. Cut baguette in half lengthwise and scoop out some of the soft crumbs inside to create a shell. Line bottom of bread shell with arugula. Top with beef slices. Set aside.

2. To prepare relish, with a very sharp knife, remove the rind and white pith from the oranges. Section the fruit by cutting between the membranes. Cut each orange section into 3 or 4 pieces. Chop the red onion, mint, cilantro, olives, and garlic, and combine with orange sections. Stir in the hot red pepper flakes.

4. Whisk together oil and lime juice. Pour over relish mixture and lightly toss. Spoon orange relish over the beef then top with other bread half. Press bread halves together. Wrap in plastic wrap and refrigerate for up to 12 hours, until ready to slice and serve.

RED POTATOES WITH BOLD TOPPINGS

Time: 35 minutes
Makes 12 pieces

Choose blemish-free baby red potatoes for these delicious snacks. The toppings could also go into large Idaho potatoes (at least ½ pound each). Bake these large potatoes at 375° for 1½ hours until the skins are very crisp. Cut them in half, and then partially scoop out and fill the skins. (Save the inside of the potatoes for another use.)

> 12 small red potatoes, about 2 pounds
> Salsa Verde (recipe follows), or
> Mustard Cheese with Bacon (recipe follows)

1. Preheat oven to 350°. Scrub potatoes and pierce each in several places with a tip of a sharp knife. Bake until tender, about 30 minutes. Transfer potatoes to a cutting board.
2. To serve, cut each potato in half. Place cut side down on a serving tray. With a melon-ball scoop, remove some of the top of each potato to create a small cavity.
3. Fill each potato with about 1 tablespoon of desired topping.

SALSA VERDE
Makes about 1 1/2 cups

8 tomatillos, husked and coarsely chopped
2 serrano chiles with seeds, finely chopped
1 small onion, finely chopped
3 tablespoons minced fresh cilantro
Juice of 1 lime
1 tablespoon olive oil
¼ cup sliced almonds
Salt, to taste

1. Husk and chop tomatillos. Chop chiles and onion. Mince cilantro.

2. Combine all ingredients.

MUSTARD CHEESE WITH BACON
Makes about 1 1/2 cups

1½ cups lightly packed shredded sharp white cheddar cheese, about 6 ounces
6 slices bacon, cooked crisp and crumbled
1 tablespoon Dijon mustard
¼ teaspoon cayenne pepper

1. Shred cheese. Cook bacon until crisp. Drain on paper towels and crumble.

2. In a small bowl, combine cheese, mustard, and cayenne. Set aside.

3. When ready to serve, preheat broiler. Spoon the cheese into each potato. Sprinkle with crumbled bacon.

4. Place filled potatoes on a baking sheet. Broil, 4 inches from source of heat, until cheese is melted and bubbling.

ROASTED CAULIFLOWER WITH HABANERO AÏOLI

Makes 4 to 6 servings
Time: 35 minutes

Dry roasting brings out the natural sweet, nutty flavor of cauli-flower. Served with a garlicky mayonnaise spiked with a smidgeon of dried habanero chile, this often bland vegetable becomes a delightful finger food.

> 1 head cauliflower (about 3 pounds)
> 3 tablespoons olive oil
> Salt and freshly ground pepper
>
> *H a b a n e r o   A ï o l i*
> 2 large egg yolks
> 3 garlic cloves, peeled
> ½ dried habanero chile, crushed (about ¼ teaspoon)
>   or ½ teaspoon cayenne pepper
> Juice of ⅔ lemon
> ¼ teaspoon salt
> 1¼ cups extra-virgin olive oil
> Salt and freshly ground pepper, to taste

1. Preheat oven to 350°. Trim and cut cauliflower into florets. Place florets in a shallow roasting pan; drizzle with olive oil and season with salt and pepper. Roast, stirring occasionally, for about 30 minutes, until cauliflower is crisp-tender and lightly browned. Using a slotted spoon, transfer cauliflower to a serving platter.
2. While cauliflower is roasting, prepare aïoli by placing egg yolks, peeled garlic cloves, chile, lemon juice, and salt in the workbowl of a food processor or blender. Process until smooth.
3. With motor running, slowing add the oil through the feed tube. Process until thick. Spoon aïoli into a small bowl and use for dipping the room-temperature cauliflower.

SANTA FE GRANOLA

Makes about 8 cups
Time: 60 minutes

This spicy breakfast cereal topped with milk is a terrific wake-up call. It's also great dry, eaten out-of-hand as a fortifier on a hiking trail or as a late-evening snack.

4 cups quick cooking oats
1 cup wheat germ
½ cup flaked unsweetened coconut
¼ cup hulled, unsalted sunflower seeds
¼ cup hulled, unsalted pumpkin seeds
1 cup coarsely chopped pecans
¼ cup pine nuts
¼ cup (½ stick) unsalted butter or margarine
2 tablespoons light brown sugar
1½ teaspoons ground cumin
1 teaspoon ground cinnamon
1 teaspoon cayenne pepper
1 cup dried cherries, dried cranberries, or raisins

1. Preheat oven to 300°. In a large, ungreased, shallow baking pan with sides, combine oats, wheat germ, coconut, sunflower seeds, pumpkin seeds, pecans, and pine nuts.

2. In a small saucepan over low heat, melt butter. Stir in brown sugar, cumin, cinnamon, and cayenne pepper. Pour over oat mixture and stir to mix well.

3. Spread mixture out evenly in pan. Bake in preheated oven for 20 to 25 minutes, stirring frequently, until golden brown. Remove from oven.

4. When cool, stir in cherries. (Store in a tightly covered jar for up to 1 week.)

SPICY MUSHROOM & GOAT CHEESE PIZZA

Makes 8 pieces
Time: 30 minutes

Ready-made, refrigerated pizza crusts are time-saving stand-ins for made-from-scratch pizza dough. If you like your pizza spicier, increase the amount of hot red pepper flakes.

1 ready-made 12- to 14-inch pizza crust, or 1 package
   (10 ounces) refrigerated pizza dough
½ tablespoon olive oil
⅛ teaspoon dried hot red pepper flakes
½ cup thinly sliced fresh mushrooms
5 sun-dried tomatoes, halved lengthwise
6 ounces goat cheese, crumbled
¼ cup chopped fresh basil

1. Preheat oven to 425°. Grease a 12- to 14-inch pizza pan. Roll or pat crust to fit prepared pan. Brush crust with olive oil and sprinkle evenly with hot red pepper flakes.

2. Slice mushrooms and arrange with sun-dried tomatoe halves over crust. Scatter goat cheese over top. Chop basil and sprinkle over top.

3. Bake in preheated oven until crust is golden brown and cheese is bubbling, 15 to 20 minutes. Cut into wedges.

SWEET ONION & CHILE PEPPER FOCACCIA

Makes about 12 pieces
Time: 90 minutes

Focaccia, the rustic flatbread for snacking from Italy, is equally delicious hot or at room temperature. Frozen bread dough gives you a head start.

> ¼ cup olive oil
> Flour
> 2 1-pound frozen white bread dough, thawed and kneaded together
> ¼ cup chopped cilantro
> ½ cup chopped walnuts
> 2 jalapeño chiles, seeded and minced
> 2 tablespoons unsalted butter
> 1 large sweet onion (Vidalia, Walla Walla, Maui, or Texas 1015 Supersweet), peeled and very thinly sliced

1. Brush a 10-by 15-inch baking pan with 1 tablespoon olive oil. Stretch and press dough into the pan, pushing it into the

sides and corners and filling the pan evenly. Drizzle 1 table-spoon olive oil over dough. Dimple the surface of the dough with your fingers.

2. Chop cilantro and walnuts. Seed and mince chiles. Combine cilantro, walnuts, and chiles and sprinkle evenly over the dough.

3. Cover the pan with plastic wrap and let stand in a warm place until dough doubles, about 40 to 50 minutes.

4. Meanwhile, preheat oven to 400°. Thinly slice onion. In a large skillet, heat remaining 2 tablespoons of olive oil over low heat. Add onion and cook, stirring occasionally, until wilted but not browned, about 5 minutes.

5. Spread onions evenly over dough. Bake in preheated oven until dough is well browned on bottom and edges, 30 to 40 minutes. Cut into small squares.

Spicy

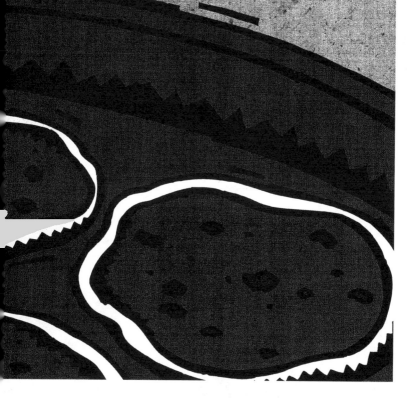

ARIZONA THREE-CHEESE FONDUE

Makes about 6 cups
Time: 20 minutes

Offer Healthy Tortilla Chips (page 40) or cubes of sourdough bread for dipping in this great fondue.

2 jalapeño chiles, seeded and minced
1 New Mexican or Anaheim green chile, seeded
    and minced
1 large red bell pepper, seeded and minced
1 medium onion, minced
2 cups shredded Jack cheese
2 cups shredded sharp white cheddar
6 ounces goat cheese, crumbled
2 tablespoons olive oil
1 teaspoon good-quality chili powder
½ teaspoon ground cumin
¼ teaspoon cayenne pepper
Minced fresh cilantro for garnish

1. Seed and mince the jalapeños, green chile, and red pepper.

Mince the onion. Grate the Jack and cheddar cheese. Crumble the goat cheese.

2. In a heavy saucepan over medium heat, sauté jalapeños, red pepper, and onion in olive oil until onion is limp, about 5 minutes.

2. Stir in the cheeses, about ¼ cup at a time, making sure cheese has melted completely before adding more cheese. Stir in chili powder, cumin, and cayenne.

3. Transfer to a chafing dish or fondue pot. Serve warm, sprinkling with chopped cilantro just before serving.

BLACK BEAN WONTONS WITH WASABI SAUCE

Makes 32 pieces
Time: 45 minutes

Wonton skins are sold fresh in Asian markets and the produce section of most supermarkets. You'll find the wasabi powder (Japanese horseradish) near the soy sauce. If unavailable, substitute prepared horseradish.

> 2 garlic cloves
> 1 cup drained canned black beans
> 1 teaspoon ground cumin
> 1 teaspoon crushed dried oregano
> 1 teaspoon good-quality chili powder
> 3 to 4 jalapeño chiles
> 32 wonton skins
> Peanut oil or canola oil, for frying
> Wasabi Sauce
> ½ cup soy sauce
> 1 tablespoon wasabi powder
> Juice of 1 lime
> 2 garlic cloves

1. Peel and quarter garlic cloves. In a food processor or blender, puree beans, garlic, cumin, oregano, and chili powder.
2. Slice jalapeño chiles into ⅛-inch thick rings. Place about ½ tablespoon of the bean mixture in the center of each wonton wrapper. Top each with a jalapeño slice.
3. Moisten edges of wrapper with water. Fold two opposite corners together over filling to form a triangle. Press edges together to seal.
4. Heat the oil to 375° in a heavy skillet or a wok (you'll need about 2 inches of oil). While oil is heating, combine all the sauce ingredients in a food processor or blender. Process until smooth. Pour into a small bowl and set aside.
5. When oil is hot, fry the wontons, a few at a time, until crisp and golden brown, about 2 minutes. Remove and drain on paper towels. Serve warm with Wasabi Sauce for dipping.

CRISPY TOFU WITH TAHINI-CILANTRO DIPPING SAUCE

Makes 4 servings
Time: 25 minutes

The fried tofu absorbs the flavor of the piquant sauce in this delightful snack. The cornstarch makes the tofu extra crispy.

1 1-pound package firm tofu
½ cup cornstarch
Peanut oil for deep-frying

Tahini Cilantro Dipping Sauce
Juice of 1½ lemons
Grated zest of ½ lemon
1 tablespoon minced fresh ginger
2 garlic cloves
1 tablespoon light brown sugar
2 tablespoons tahini
¼ cup lightly packed cilantro leaves
Dash liquid hot pepper sauce
2 tablespoons dark sesame oil
½ cup peanut oil

1. Drain tofu and cut into 1-inch cubes. Pat tofu dry with paper towels and coat cubes with cornstarch.

2. In a large, heavy-bottom skillet or wok, heat peanut oil over medium-high heat until hot.

3. Add tofu cubes and cook until golden brown and crispy on all sides, 8 to 10 minutes. Remove and drain on paper towels.

4. Meanwhile, mince ginger. In a food processor or blender, combine all of the sauce ingredients except peanut oil until smooth. With motor running, slowly add peanut oil. Process until smooth and thick.

5. To serve, arrange tofu cubes on a serving platter. Pour sauce into a small bowl for dipping.

RINGS OF FIRE

Makes 4 servings
Time: 30 minutes

For those truly crazy about hot chiles!

> 2 poblano chiles
> 2 jalapeño chiles
> 2 New Mexican or Anaheim chiles
> 2 serrano chiles
> 1½ cups unbleached all-purpose flour
> ¼ cup stoneground cornmeal
> 1 teaspoon salt
> 1 cup buttermilk
> Canola oil, for frying

1. Cut all of the chiles into ⅛-inch thick rings. In a small bowl, combine flour, cornmeal, and salt. Dust chile rings with flour mixture. Dip into buttermilk, then again into the flour mixture.

2. Heat oil in a heavy-bottom skillet or wok to 375˚. Drop a few of the prepared chiles into hot oil. Cook until lightly browned. Remove and drain on paper towels. Repeat until all chiles are cooked. Serve warm.

SPICY COUSCOUS WITH ALMONDS IN LETTUCE WRAP-UPS

Makes 1 serving
Time: 15 minutes

A quick, healthy afternoon snack that won't spoil appetites for dinner.

½ teaspoon minced fresh ginger
¼ cup chicken stock
1 teaspoon fresh lemon juice
1 teaspoon unsalted butter or margarine
½ teaspoon curry powder
⅛ teaspoon cayenne pepper
2 tablespoons quick-cooking couscous
2 ripe olives, sliced

1 tablespoon sliced almonds
1 ounce feta cheese, crumbled
2 large leaves of green leaf lettuce, washed and crisped

1. Mince the ginger. In a small saucepan, bring chicken broth, lemon juice, butter, ginger, curry powder, and cayenne pepper to a boil. Stir in couscous.
2. Cover and remove from heat. Let stand for 5 minutes, until couscous absorbs all of the broth. Fluff with a fork.
3. Stir in olives, almonds, and feta cheese. Scoop couscous into lettuce leaves to eat.

TEXAS PECAN PANCAKES WITH CRÈME FRAÎCHE & JALAPEÑO JELLY

Makes about 20 3-inch pancakes
Time: 25 minutes

Be sure to buy a good quality, not too sweet, jalapeño jelly with plenty of "heat" for these delicious little pancakes. A lovely, spicy way to start a lazy Sunday!

1 cup toasted pecans
4 large eggs
2 cups half & half
⅓ cup sugar
4 teaspoons baking powder
2½ cups unbleached all-purpose flour
¼ teaspoon salt
½ teaspoon cornstarch
Unsalted butter
Crème fraîche, for topping (see box)
Jalapeño jelly, for topping

1. To toast pecans, preheat oven to 375°. Spread whole pecans halves in a single layer in a shallow baking pan. Bake for about 10 minutes, stirring once or twice, until pecans are fragrant and crisp. Remove from pan and cool to room temperature. Coarsely chop.

2. Meanwhile, in a mixing bowl, whisk together eggs and half & half. Whisk in sugar.

3. Combine baking powder, flour, salt, and cornstarch. Gradually sift flour mixture into egg mixture, whisking constantly. When combined (the mixture with be quite thin and runny), stir in pecans.

4. Working in batches, spoon batter, using about 2 tablespoons of the batter per pancake, onto a hot, buttered pancake griddle or large skillet. Cook until brown on the bottom and steam holes appear on the top. Turn and cook about two minutes longer, until cooked through and lightly browned. Repeat with remaining batter, buttering the griddle between batches as necessary. Serve hot with a dollop of crème fraîche and jalapeño jelly.

CRÈME FRAÎCHE
Makes 1 cup

You can find crème fraîche in the dairy sections of many supermarkets or you can make your own ahead of time by whisking together ½ cup heavy cream and ½ cup sour cream. Transfer to a covered glass jar and let stand in a warm place for 12 hours. Chill for 24 hours before using. Keeps refrigerated for up to 1 week.

THAI SPRING ROLLS WITH SASSY GINGER SAUCE

Makes 48 pieces
Time: 90 minutes

A combination of shrimp, pork, fresh vegetables, and spices, these delectable morsels are wrapped in crispy rice paper and served with a fresh ginger dipping sauce. Fresh rice papers are sold in Asian markets and some supermarkets. Sealed in a plastic bag, they'll keep at room temperature for several months.

½ pound peeled small shrimp, chopped
2 ounces fresh shiitake mushrooms, minced, or ¼ ounce dried shiitake mushrooms, soaked in warm water for 20 minutes, drained, and minced
1 medium onion, minced
2 garlic cloves, minced
1 medium carrot, shredded
¼ cup chopped cilantro
¼ pound ground fresh pork
¼ pound fresh bean sprouts
½ teaspoon freshly ground pepper
48 6-inch rice papers

Lukewarm water
Peanut or canola oil, for frying

Sassy Ginger Sauce
1 cup soy sauce
⅓ cup red wine vinegar
1½ tablespoons minced fresh ginger

1. Peel and chop shrimp. Chop fresh or soaked dried mushrooms. Mince onion and garlic. Shred carrot. Chop cilantro.
2. In a medium bowl, combine shrimp, pork, mushrooms, onion, garlic, carrot, bean sprouts, cilantro, and pepper.
3. Place 1 rice paper on a flat work surface. (Keep remaining rice papers covered with plastic wrap to prevent them from drying out and curling up.)
4. Place 2 teaspoons of shrimp mixture near a corner edge. Fold that corner edge over the filling. Fold the right side corner over the filling, then fold over the left side corner. Roll and tightly seal. Set aside and continue to fill each rice paper. Repeat until all rice papers are filled.
5. Heat oil in a large heavy-bottom skillet or wok to 375˚. While oil is heating, combine all the sauce ingredients. Pour into a small bowl. Set aside.
6. When oil is hot, fry 5 or 6 spring rolls at a time until golden brown on all sides, about 5 to 7 minutes. Remove and drain on paper towels. Serve warm with Sassy Ginger Sauce for dipping.

ZUCCHINI FRITTERS WITH MINT SAUCE

Makes about 24 fritters
Time: 30 minutes

A delectable way to use the bounty of zucchini from your garden.

1 teaspoon minced fresh ginger
2 tablespoons minced fresh flat-leaf parsley
1 large carrot, peeled and shredded
3 medium zucchini, about 1 pound total, coarsely
   shredded
1 cup unbleached all-purpose flour
1 large egg
Juice of 1 lemon
5 tablespoons water
1 teaspoon fresh thyme leaves or ¼ teaspoon
crushed dried
½ teaspoon salt

Freshly ground pepper, to taste
Canola oil, for frying

M i n t   S a u c e
2 tablespoons minced onion
½ cup loosely packed fresh mint leaves, minced
1 cup plain low-fat yogurt

1. Mince the ginger and parsley. Peel and shred the carrots. Shred the zucchini.
2. In a large bowl, mix together flour, egg, lemon juice, and water until smooth. Stir in thyme, ginger, parsley, salt, pepper, zucchini, and carrot. Set aside.
3. In a heavy-bottom skillet, heat 1 inch of oil over medium heat. While oil is heating, mince onions and mint leaves and combine with yogurt in a small bowl. Set aside.
4. When oil is hot, drop 3 or 4 fritters into the skillet, using a heaping tablespoon of batter per fritter. Cook until golden on the bottom, about 1½ minutes. Turn and continue to cook until crispy and golden brown, about 1½ minutes. Remove and drain on paper towels.
4. Repeat with remaining batter, adding oil as needed to the skillet. When all fritters are cooked, arrange on a heated serving platter. Garnish each with a dollop of mint sauce.

LIQUID AND DRY MEASURE EQUIVALENCIES

Customary	Metric
¼ teaspoon	1.25 milliliters
½ teaspoon	2.5 milliliters
1 teaspoon	5 milliliters
1 tablespoon	15 milliliters
1 fluid ounce	30 milliliters
¼ cup	60 milliliters
⅓ cup	80 milliliters
½ cup	120 milliliters
1 cup	240 milliliters
1 pint (2 cups)	680 milliliters
1 quart (4 cups; 32 ounces)	960 milliliters (.96 liter)
1 gallon (4 quarts)	3.84 liters
1 ounce (by weight)	28 grams
¼ pound (4 ounces)	114 grams
1 pound (16 ounces)	454 grams
2.2 pounds	1 kilogram (1,000 grams)

OVEN TEMPERATURE EQUIVALENTS

Description	°Fahrenheit	°Celsius
Cool	200	90
Very slow	250	120
Slow	300-325	150-160
Moderately slow	325-350	160-180
Moderate	350-375	180-190
Moderately hot	375-400	190-200
Hot	400-450	200-230
Very hot	450-500	230-260

Printed in the United States
By Bookmasters